A Seeker's Journey

Reflections of Enlightenment

Compiled By

Najwa Haamen

"Life isn't about finding yourself, it's about creating and being willing to walk into your truths designated uniquely for you"

~Najwa (The Brown Eyed Poet)

CONTENTS

INTRODUCTION

————————————)( )(————————————

Thank you for taking the time to even buy this book, let alone read it! Throughout the early stages of writing this, I had a lot of people ask me what exactly is the book about? The only way I could answer this question is by expressing my reasoning for writing it.

Being raised as a Muslim, I never personally got to have the experience of what it was like to leave a religion or different spiritual practice and not just seek out but accept Islam. I only know what it is like to grow up and into myself as a Muslim. There is no regret here because my life as a Muslim has been quite the journey, Alhumdulillah (all praise be to Allah), but when I would listen to other's journey to Islam, there was always a feeling of admiration I felt toward them. The entire process of questioning, wondering, feelings of loss, the seeking and accepting of a completely different way of life is both beautiful and courageous. The process of conversion/reversion is so inspiring to me; people leaving everything they lived or practiced for something completely different in ways of practice and lifestyle is a story I felt needed to be shared.

In gathering my stories, just reading, speaking and interacting with the different people that I know in real life, has taken me on a life journey of my own. I appreciate everyone who took a chance and believed in my vision. You trusted me with your life story and I pray that I presented it well. So my sole intent behind this book is, to share that beauty with all who will read it and InShaa Allah (Allah willing), give people a different perspective, understanding and create a tolerance for differences. Please read with an open mind and open heart, I pray you enjoy it. In order for you to truly understand my inspiration for this book, I need to introduce you to where I come from...

RAUSHANAH

———————————————×( )×———————————————

When my daughter asked me to be in her book, I was a little hesitant to even give a synopsis of my story. I do not like talking about myself. However, I gave a concerted effort to give an accurate account of what led me to practicing this religion I love.

I was so-call raised to believe that Jesus was the "Son of God", believing that he had died for our sins and that there was "The Father, Son and the Holy Ghost" whomever that was, as a way of life; typical for most black folks. But as I became more aware of the world around me, I became increasingly dissatisfied with that understanding. I was not sure what this belief system was because in my household that included my mother, my sister and brothers, we did not practice any type of church-going regularly, nor praying together unless it was a recognized holiday in which it was expected that you would go to church, i.e. "Easter" or "Good Friday"; The days that all good Christians go to church and do communion by symbolizing the ritual of taking a piece of white cracker as the body of Jesus and some red grape juice as the blood to drink. I could never understand why we had to do this but when you don't know any better you do what you are taught and follow the masses. We never read the stories from the Bible that was in our house and my mother was never home to give us any guidance in morality. She did not have the skills, which I did not know at that time, or the understanding of what it took to be the leader of her children to understand the Christian religion. If the information did not come from various relatives or the television, there were no real formal teachings of the Bible. We practiced the ritual of Christmas but it was not from a spiritual sense just from a traditional sense. That expectation of doing what others would do during this time. Anything I've learned about Christianity I'd learned through the lenses of the outside world and not from my household.

I was born in 1955 during the Civil Rights era in Philadelphia, Pa. I was among the first of my cousins to be born in the Germantown area in a house that included my mother's mother and Aunts. We moved to the North Philadelphia area when I was about 4 years old along with my sister and brother, me being the oldest of the three, I was given the task of being the responsible one for my siblings as my mother navigated her way through her life, all the time not really knowing how I fit in this world. At the age of 6 I was violated by my Uncle Lucky, my Aunt Sis husband on Christmas at her house and that is where my world stopped. I will never forget that day nor all of the atrocities of what was happening around the country that I really didn't understand. I witnessed the killing of John F. Kennedy, Martin Luther King, Malcolm X (Malcolm Little), Madger Evers, and many of the Civil Rights uproars that was displayed on the television. My mother did not give any account of what was really happening to us and I really didn't know why. I grew up poor, sometimes not having enough food, heat or the necessities of life. As I became older and more aware of my surroundings I began to understand my role as a black girl, young teenager and woman. I became a mother as a young teenager at 15 years old. Wow what a life-changing experience that was. But it only was a continuation of what role my mother had groomed me for. Although she'd help with raising my child and allowed me to finish school I still had the responsibility of raising another human being that I was not ready for. I stayed in my mother's home until I turned 18 years old and I moved out on my own with no real resources to survive. I was a welfare mom with a child and no skills to lead a better life than the one I'd left. I am forever grateful for the help my Mom had given me. Without her I would've been a drug addict and only Allah knows best what else. She was there even when I was a nut not knowing what else to do.

When I left home it was then that I became aware of the different ideologies and versions of the truth according to other Black people. There was the Nation of Islam through the leadership of the Honorable Elijah Muhammad, the Moorish- Americans through the leadership of Noble Drew Ali, The 5%ers with 95% of Christianity and 5% of Islam, The Hebrew Israelites who would talk about the original people of the bible were black, the followers of Marcus Garvey; you name it was well and alive in Philadelphia. Although these organizations were around when I was a young child I did not become aware of them until I got out on my own. Most of these organizations were born before or during the Civil Rights era, and I had no clue what it all meant. I do know that Islam through the Nation of Islam appealed to me. I was mesmerized by the illusion of structure and order that was the face of this black movement thinking that it was going to help bring black people together to build an actual nation. However, I was unaware of the numerous times that black people had the wealth to build a separate nation but white people would somehow just take it away from us, rendering us back to needing and depending on the systemic structure of white supremacy.

My cousin Samimah was living with a man by the name of Hassan. He was a member of the Nation of Islam. It was through numerous talks with him that I learned about the Nation. The Nation for me was a safe haven from all of the misunderstandings that I had about the world. I went on to become a member of this organization by obtaining my "X", which is to symbolize you as a person of a lost nation. I became Shcila 34X. Wow, how was I going to present myself to the world around me? What did it all mean? Even though I had done what was required to get this letter "X", what now? In my everyday life I was still on paper Sheila Williams (Bey). I still had to conduct all of my business dealings in that name. I could not go around and say I was Sheila 34X. That name was only used when I went to the Temple. So I continued on my journey to seeking the truth that would appeal to my understanding of the world, even though my fear of the unknown always lurked in the back of my mind. But because I did not know that it was fear I struggled to uplift myself and follow my dreams. I lacked motivation to pursue a life that I always wanted. I always dreamed of being a doctor. I always wanted to help others through whatever struggles that they were going through but I did not know how. Moving forward I delved into becoming the best Muslim that I could be. Although I didn't know much about the various sects of Islam, I bounced from one ideology to another to another even though I became a member of the Nation of Islam. My grandmother on my father's side had been a member of the Moorish Science Temple of Islam under the teachings of the Noble Drew Ali, so because I was familiar with her I decided to see what that was about, but not on my own. I had become involved with my oldest son's father and he was a part of this movement which meant that I did it because of him. Boy was I gullible. That did not work out well. From there I went back to the Nation of Islam which had now become the Bilalian community. Although all of this took place all while having on again off again relationships I had continued to stay consistent with my journey towards what I wanted and that was my understanding of the truth as I perceived it. On day as I was standing in front of the Sister Clara Muhammad School on the corner of 47th and Wylausing St. I heard a sound that I had never heard before. It was coming from another building across the street, about half a block away. It was the most beautiful and extremely heart penetrating melody that I had ever heard. It said Allahu Akbar, Allahu Akbar!!! I don't remember who I was talking to but I turned to that person and said "what is that?" I don't quite remember what was said but I followed that sound from across the street. And so began my personal journey to what I believed to be the true religion of (GOD) ALLAH, the religion that I now have come to know as Sunni Islam, believing in the Oneness of ALLAH and the teachings of Prophet Muhammad, Salla Allahu Alaihi Was Salaam(May the peace and many blessings of Allah be upon him). To ALLAH I am ever grateful for striving in this direction even though the path was dark and confusing at times. The many twists and turns that are paved in this path of truth only helped me to become closer to ALLAH. I would not have traded this journey for anything else. May ALLAH continue to provide me with HIS guidance upon this journey back to HIM. AMEEN.

TAJ

———————————————— ✳ ✳ ————————————————

My journey to Islam is quite interesting and it all really started when I was six years old. Going to Sunday school, I was not able to grasp the concept of God being a man (Jesus) but also hearing Jesus is the son of God. At that age, I couldn't verbally put my words together to express my confusion, I just knew that I wouldn't practice the Christianity way of life; but I did believe in Santa Claus , so go figure! Over the years I remember my mother dabbling into several different religions, from Non Denominational Christianity, witchcraft to Buddhism and everything else in between; so, I am quite versed in a lot of anthropology, religious or non religious practices. Although my family associated themselves with Christiannity, we weren't strict on practicing any specific way of life, which allowed me to never really give religion an in-depth thought.

Once I turned twelve years old, my parents were comfortable with me going to church by myself on Sundays. When neither of them could attend, my job was to write down the scriptures and narrate what the pastor spoke about that day. However, I had different plans once I arrived; I'd walk in to be handed "today's schedule", go find a seat, sit a minute, then walk right back out and "pretend" I had to go to the bathroom. Once the coast was clear, I would leave and run to my friend's house who was only a few blocks away. While I visit her I would think of a topic that I could talk about, scour the Bible to find verses similar to my "topic". I must say every time I had to do this, I got away with it. When asked about the sermon, I was fluid in my explanation, strangely it was believable; like when I say I had zero interest in religion and didn't want to become an official Christian, I was dead serious. However, after attending church alone a few times, out of the blue my mother said she wanted me to get baptized. I did not want to do that because for one, it felt forced and two, I didn't want to commit my life to Christ. The day my mom scheduled my baptism, I went alone because she wasn't able to make it, go figure. Since this was going to be a solo journey to my own baptism, I decided not to go and avoid the entire process altogether. My only stop was to my girlfriend's house five blocks away from the church. I stayed over her house for at least two hours, and then went home. Once I got home I literally had to lie and tell my mom they cancelled and would announce a future date; oddly enough she let it go and did no further investigation.

Fast forward some years, we moved further on the south side of Chicago and interestingly enough the famous, well known Nation of Islam Mosque called the Mosque Maryam, was only four blocks away from where we moved. One day, my dad and I went to the pizza joint directly across the street from Mosque Maryam, it was a Sunday, and while we waited for our order looked out the window. All I saw were these beautiful covered women and said to my dad, "I am going to be one of those ladies, one day." He laughed and said, "Sweetheart in due time, in due time." His calm approach about my curiosity of considering a different religion which clearly, by modest attire makes you stand out, had me even more intrigued. In a really strange way, life agreed with my father and because I was already on a deadly path before ending at Islam. When I turned thirteen years old, I joined a violent, native roots gang- the Gangsta Disciples; what lead me down this path is an entirely different story but let's just say my childhood was not perfect in the least and from a young child, I was exposed to the street lifestyle such as drugs, gangs, violence and murder. At the point of discovering the Nation of Islam, I had already been an active gang member two solid years, reaching a decent status in dope dealing and earning my respect. Despite the recognition and respect I had earned, I always felt like something was missing and never felt spiritually fulfilled. I often ignored this feeling because all I knew were the religions I was taught or pagan beliefs and had no desire to seek comfort in any of them.

During my freshman year of high school I was cutting classes, skipping days altogether, getting into fights, the textbook juvenile delinquency behavior which eventually caught up with me. The school board contacted my parents, who were separated at the time, letting them know that I was on the verge of expulsion and something had to change. My parents agreed amongst themselves it would be best to transfer me to a different school to start over, preferably a Catholic high school that would provide some form of academic discipline and religious structure. Looking back, it was the best decision they made because Chicago public high school in the 90's was a major distraction to the youth if you weren't academically driven. Over the summer they applied to two all girl high schools but I was denied due to attendance and subpar grades; one more attempt and the Academy of Our Lady was my new high school. Sister Maryam (go figure), established some ground rules and I was enrolled. I was still gang affiliated but I knew I couldn't bring any of that on school grounds and skipping classes was not an option because tuition was being paid for my attendance. Eventually, I had to sit down with the Regent for my block to discuss rearranging my days to sell, be on the streets for lookouts, etc.

Growing up in the early 90's Black consciousness in Hip Hop was on the rise with Public Enemy, Poor Righteous Teachers, Dead Prez, X-Clan just to name a few, this was highly influential music to the youth of that era, especially for me. Listening to these MCs, I was given a preview of a mindset aside from the street/gang violence; the positive words uplifted me. I was mentally torn between doing what was right and enjoying what was wrong, making money at the same time. Keeping those beautifully covered sisters in my memory, I began to agree that all Black people needed to rise up. I knew the street life was tearing communities apart and destroying ourselves and families but when you are making close to a stack ($1000) a night- the wrong thing to do is easily excusable. Being in Catholic school and noticing all of my history classes, from Freshman year to Senior year, taught nothing related to African American history, I mean since the school was predominantly Black girls. Why couldn't we learn about ourselves if we must learn about everyone else? We have our own history, a history that should be told. So, naturally, my leadership role came into play and I requested African American history be taught and applied as a prerequisite for credit at school. I was told by the Vice Principal that in order to get the class accepted I needed to have 200 signatures from the students. Over the course of a week I got my signatures and the school was forced to find a teacher to teach the class. Talk about feeling like I made some form of good change!

After about four weeks of waiting for the class to be up and running, on the weekends I found myself at the Mosque Maryam listening to Farrakhan speak and prepping to become a MGT. What I found interesting, a lot of teen and young adults who joined the FOI and MGT were either active gang members or just getting out of a gang. The rule in any gang in Chicago was blood in-blood out, so the exception to this rule would be you joining the Nation of Islam because of the respect they gained all over the city. Their due diligence to improve the conditions within the black communities and decrease crime was respected by everyone, gang affiliated and non. I paid for my MGT uniform, which was all white like the ones I had seen looking out of that pizza store window that day and passed the physical and written exam. I was so happy and felt honored to be amongst my people doing something positive for myself. Once my school established the African American class with a teacher and a textbook, it was time to learn! About a week into the class there was a girl that sat in front me in class who notice my "Pro Black" vibe and said, "I have a boyfriend whose brother is a Muslim, but he believes anyone can be a Muslim." I looked at her perplexed, with a frown on my face, I said, "Oh really, give me his number." In the back of my mind I was like I will tell dude a thing or two when we talk! To me it felt like weeks went by before she finally gave me his number. Once I got home, I immediately called him, I remember his name… Brother Ishmael. Alhumdulillah, he was a sincere brother that was truly giving dawah. We talked for a week (from Thursday to Wednesday), everything he explained from Tawheed (the Oneness of God), the Quran, the Bible, Jesus, Muhammad (peace and blessings be upon him), it all made sense and for the first time in my life I didn't have doubts or questions; it was crystal clear amd things felt right. The next day my school had arranged a field trip for us to go see the movie Malcolm X in theaters. I was so emotionally moved by that movie, I bought the autobiography. I called Ishmael and told him I was ready to take my Shahaadah (testimony of Faith) and we decided that Friday was the perfect day. I was able to sneak out of school without notice, met up with him and he took me to his home where his fiancee was waiting. Don't ask me why I trusted a stranger, I just felt in that moment that I could trust him. We arrived at his home, after introductions and some small talk, with verbal instruction, I took my Shahaadah at sixteen years old! It was also Ramadhan so I was able to fast the remaining two weeks! Allahu Akbar (Allah is the Greatest)! From that day forward, I never looked back. I got out of the gang and slowly began practicing Islam. For me, it was the best decision I ever made. I love being Muslim. I love representing for the Muslim woman and the simplicity of our belief. I have learned and experienced so much over the last 25 years and I wouldn't change a thing because all experiences lead to great wisdom. May Allah the Most High continue to guide me and keep me on His straight path Ameen! I am blessed, I feel grateful and I look forward to many more decades as a Muslim by His Mercy. Allah is Most Kind, Oft-forgiving and Most Merciful.

RACHEL

———————×( )×———————

S o, I was raised as a Jehovah's Witness. Then as I grew older, after getting kicked out of my house as a teen, I stopped any sort of faith pretty much. I went on a rebellious streak for about eight to ten years. A life filled with "fun sins", drinking, smoking, fornication, etc. A wild and extreme period of my existence. As a child in a highly dysfunctional family, I suffered from feelings of self loathing and depression pretty much early on in life. I was diagnosed with bi-polar depression around the age of twenty or twenty-one. I have taken several different antidepressants that all left me numb from emotion of any sort. I didn't like feeling like this. At around the age of twenty-two I felt a strong urge to find spirituality. It was an instinct, I couldn't shake. I felt like a religion would give me some sort of comfort. But it had to be the right religion though.

I didn't believe that my childhood religion was correct because of a few factors, one being the would "disfellowship" members of the congregation when they sinned. Meaning no one could talk to them for months on end. My mother was disfellowshipped before and I remember feeling so badly for her when we went to meetings. Anyhow, I also wasn't sure about Jesus as the son of God (or God) idea. But, because I didn't know much about Islam and most of the people I knew were Christian, I still gravitated towards Christiantiy in my quest. I visited different churches and read up on all sorts of religions. The only thing I knew about Islam was that the women had to cover, they also had to wear a face veil if they were married (an ignorant psuedo fact that floats around to this day), and that the men could have more than one wife. That was about it. So one day I got a book called "Islam for Dummies". The book laid out the facts of the religion in a simple manner and was very well written in my opinion. I highlighted the things that interested me most. It seemed to all make sense to me so I decided that I would try Islam. But I wasn't ready or so I thought. I thought that I needed to stop my "fun sins" first before taking my Shahaadah.

A few weeks later, I went to family court and saw a brother I somewhat knew who sold oils. He would also try to convince me to be a Muslim. I would always tell him no thanks. But this time I was really listening as he was talking. I told him thoughts of how I wanted to be righteous before I committed. He told me something that always stuck with me. He asked me what would happen if I died tomorrow and hadn't yet submitted to Allah? The consequences could be detrimental. He also said that I should do it now and that the sinning would eventually fall off. That made a lot of sense to me. So I took my Shahaadah with him as my witness. It was a slow process initially. I didn't offer salah (prayer) but it was always on my mind that I needed to and then one day I did. It was the best gift I could've ever gotten in this life. The peace that comes with Islam is unexplainable. Also the healing that can happen as you learn and try your very best to live by the teachings of the prophets and the speech of Allah in the Quran cannot be measured. My bi-polar depression left me, by Allah. My life has never been more peaceful, even through the heavy trials. I thank Allah for giving me Islam. I wish I could convince everyone in this world to learn Islam and I pray for their guidance. Alhumdulillah!

VINCENT

—————————————————————)( )(—————————————————————

O   k, where do I start? I would love for this to come out perfectly but it
        doesn't seem to always work out that way.

Islam saved my life or savd me from losing my mind. I think I was working a dead-end job at Home Depot; everything was going down-hill. I was struggling to take care of my family and I was trying to find myself as a person for the first time. I started to get into the Black Power movement. I started reading books by the Black Panthers and so on. Eventually it led me to watch the movie Malcolm X. I loved how black people were united in the film. The most powerful scene in the movie was, when Malcolm and a group of brothers from the Nation of Islam was ouside of a jail house, demanding to see a brother to make sure their brother was healthy. That scene later ended when Malcolm turned his hand and commanded the large group of men to leave. A white cop, upon seeing this said, "That's too much power for one nigga to have." At that moment I became fascinated with whatever Islam was.

I worked the night shift at Home Depot. There were about three Muslims but none of them ever gave me dawah or said much about Islam in general. There was another man that was Muslim but not practicing (if that even makes sense). Well one day an African man that was Christian was talking about the struggle of black people in America. The African said that the only thing that could unite African Americans in the United States, and the government knew and feared this, was Islam. I overheard this while eating lunch; this is what I wanted to hear. A few weeks later, I hit rock bottom and was ready to do something stupid. I happen to see one of the Muslim brothers from the job, the one not practicing, I walked up to him where he was working with tear in my eyes and asked him, "Are you a Muslim?" He stopped working and said to me, "Yes but I'm not Nation of Islam." That was amazing that he said that because before that moment, I was leading towards joining the Nation of Islam but, couldn't find a temple to hear anyone speak. When the brother told me that he wasn't in the Nation of Islam, it was like Allah guiding me from the wrong and towards the truth. The brother asked me did I want to know more about true Islam, I said yes. The nest day he brings me pamphlets about Orthodox Islam, the Prophet Muhammad (peace and blessings be upon him), the difference in Farrakhan Islam and the true Islam. He also gave me a small book of hadiths and a English translation of the Quran. The best thing he told me was that Islam was based on one's intentions. He then tells me a story that explains what he meant. At that moment, I was really interested in knowing more so I took all of my gifts and started to do my research.

I read a lot and learned a lot. I think everything was a slow process over the course of a year. I loved what I read but I just wasn't sure what to do next. I later got a new job. I felt like God was putting me on a better path. I wasn't sure which way to go but I felt the black woman that helped me get a job, might be a sign, she was a Christian. I was in search of God at the time. I said to myself that whatever church she went to, I would join. When asked what church or denomination she was with, she mentioned something that I didn't know and that didn't settle well in my heart. I was ready to become a Christian but I didn't feel it. Later, while I was working the new job, I met a guy named Askia. He was an African American man that also taught martial arts. I always wanted trai but I wanted my teacher to be black. He happened to be not only black but Muslim. I was convinced this was a sign to be Muslim. Him and I talked a lot about religion and he explained everything I needed to know. He gave me videos by Khalil Yasin and I felt really good. I think I was almost ready to take my Shahaadah, I just had to visit my father in Virginia first.

Before my trip, I decided to take a trip to a local Islamic book store to buy a new Quran to read. My plan was to visit my father and when I came back, then take my Shahaadah. When I walked into the store, I asked the owner if they sell Qurans? He asked me if I was Muslim, I said no. He then directed me to the Qurans. He started to give me dawah and asked if I was ready to take my Shahaadah. I smiled because I knew I was ready but I wanted to visit my father first. He then explained how all of my sins would gone and I would be protected if I were to take my Shahaadah that day and something happened to me. Lol! So, I started thinking about the trip I had planned to go see my dad. I felt that if something did happen to me, I would be on the right side because I took my Shahaadah. At first, I was hesitant but after some more thinking, I said this is what I want and what I need. Right then and there, I raised my right index finger and testified, " Ashadu an la illaha illa Allah, wa ashadu ana Muhammadur Rasulullah (I bear witness that there is no God or deity worthy of worship except Allah and I bear witness that Muhammad is the Messenger of Allah)."

It was the moment that changed my life for the better and I have nobody but Allah to thank for that!

JENELL

────────◀ ◯ ▶────────

I've always been a religious person. I was the only child in the house that didn't mind going to church. One reason is, I loved putting my good clothes on, Lol! The other reason is because I used to pray that my mom would get better and come back to get me so we could live like regular families. That never happened but I always felt God.

My aunt converted to Islam and I would watch her make wudhu (cleasing before prayer) and pray; from there i became intrigued. I asked a lot of questions as a child and was always very curious. Then my cousins were Muslim, my sister/cousin and I spent a lot of time around them. I just really admired their religion. As I grew older, to me, Muslim women were held at this high level and respected; I wanted that. They also seemed so disciplined and highly confident. So, I started making wudhu and praying with my aunt, just following her movements and asking questions afterwards.

My call to Islam really came when I moved with another relative and their entire family was Muslim. Then, my soon to be best friend was Muslim, along with her entire family. I loved the humbleness of her mother and the more I learned, the more I believed Islam was for me. My first Eid made it official for me, that I chose the correct path. I loved the feeling of being amongst other Muslims.

I struggle with covering but that doesn't take from my belief. I'm actually considering the niqab when I do return to wearing the hijab. I took the time away from studying but when I returned, I began to understand life and Allah better. I accepted the fact that Islam is not just a religion, it's a lifestyle. I've become very content with the Qadr (Allah's Will) after some life changing experiences. Without Islam teaching me this, I would've sunk into a deep dark place, Alhumdulillah.

Lastly, I've always felt like Allah was going to forever have me, He knows my heart and my intent. Allah guides whom He wills and I was guided so, I know this was the right decision for me.

AMIRAH

———⟩( )⟨———

I remember being eight years old and a cousin of mine died. We were at what I didn't know, at the time from being raised Baptist, to be his Janazah (Islamic funeral). Traditional funerals always left me shaken and terrified for weeks after but this special funeral brought a calmness over me; I wasn't afraid at all; in fact I felt peace. This would be the planted seed that would have me question my faith six years later at the age of fourteen. A close cousin of mine had just begun reading the Quran and studying about Islam; this fueled my zeal to learn about the religion. I purchased a Quran that I would desperately hide while I was in the house. I was so afraid that if my mother found the Quran I was reading, she would throw it away; which ultimately wound up happening. I was completely heart broken and sad but I didn't let this deter me from learning about Islam. I continued to read over the years following but it wasn't until I was nineteen years old, that I actually took my Shahaadah. It just all made sense to me. Everything I had been taught to know or questioned about Christianity, was somehow dismantled and the truth became clear by Islam. For years, I followed my mother in being a Christian and struggling with my doubts about the trinity, blindly following. However, the order, the peace, the love and mercy I read about Allah having for His slaves, is what drove me to accept Islam into my heart as a complete way of life. It gave me purpose and I felt I'd finally knew what I was placed on earth to do… worship Allah.

LAYLAH

———————————— ✕ ◯ ✕ ————————————

I have always been curious about Islam. I can recall in my younger years, my mom taking me to the DC Convention Center to hear minister Louis Farrakhan speak. My mom also lived near Howard University, so the opportunity to encounter Muslims was high. Growing up right off of Georgia Avenue in DC, literally steps from Howard, meant that as I got off the bus or metro, I may run into a brother selling oils, or brothers from the Nation of Islam selling bean pies and Final Calls. At the time that I was going to see the minister, I had no idea the difference between Orthodox Islam and the Nation of Islam. I just knew that there was something very intriguing about the "Muslims" I encountered all the time in my travels during those times. They were always well dressed, well- spoken and well mannered. Over the years, as I reached adulthood, I had even dated a few "Muslim" guys along the way. Of course, they were not practicing Islam like they should have been but even in that, they hesitated to tell me about Islam; this is when I begin to learn the difference between Orthodox Islam and the Nation of Islam.

Somewhere around the age of twenty-eight, twenty nine, I don't recall exactly, I had a spiritual awakening. This awakening was so deep that I was having nightmares and started to feel "dirty" regardless of how many times I bathed, I felt dirty. One day, I was in my apartment and I woke up but I felt something standing on my chest and I couldn't move. I felt weird energy or a "spirit" around me. Shortly thereafter, one night, I had what can now be described as an anxiety attack. Life had simply become too much and I just broke down. To this day, I do not know how I got to my grandmother's house who lived nine city blocks away from my apartment at the time; I just knew that I was at her front door in the middle of the night ringing her door bell. When she opened the door, I literally fell into her and begged her to move back home with her. I told her I would pay her whatever she wanted each month but that I needed to be around somebody I trusted and I loved. Prior to this and prior to my moving to my apartment, I had been in a toxic relationship from the time I was twenty-five until I was twenty- eight. My moving to this apartment was my fresh start. Anyway, my grannie was concerned about me and she said, "Of course you can move back in." That night, I stayed upstairs in my old room. I did not leave that room for almost a week, I slept. Woke up in buckets of sweat, changed and slept again. If anyone has seen the movie 'Ray' when he went to detox, and he was sweating, having flashbacks during his sleep; this is the only way I can describe the process I went through that week. The only difference is, I was not detoxing from drugs or alcohol but it was a detox nonetheless. During that time, my grannie didn't bother me. It was as if she knew what I was doing and she let the process happen.

I stayed with grannie until I turned thirty. I had a thirtieth birthday party at a local club in DC. Shortly after that, I had become tired of the club scene. I mean, I had only been partying since I was eighteen, if not before. I was done with it. It was in those times I started spending a lot of time alone. I would ride my bike for miles through the city and end up at the bookstores. I would read about various religions. I had grown up Christian and so I simply deferred back to that. I started going back to church and even got baptized. I had joined my mom's new church and was attending new member's courses when a Deacon in charge of the class said something inappropriate to me. It made me feel so uncomfortable. However, that was the start to my questioning the Christian religion. Every Sunday, I would go to church and sit in the balcony. You would be surprised at what you can see from the balcony of a church. I started noticing a lot of hypocrisy in the actions of the people. I would notice how women would sit on the front row, right beside the pastor's wife and open their legs- they were wearing skirts. I would notice how if an attractive woman walked by, the pastor would turn his attention to their backsides, FROM THE PULPIT!!! Here this man was preaching the word of God and he lacked basic self control. Don't get me wrong, I don't expect anyone to be perfect but I feel that a man of his caliber should have some level of self- control or respect for God; especially in the house of God. And the same for those women that were trying to tempt him on the front row. These things coupled with the "deacon" being totally inappropriate with me, made me question the religion. I went back to my childhood and how I would ask certain questions about God and Jesus and no one could really explain it to me, or when I asked where in the Bible did it say that you give 10% of your earnings, no one could show it to me! I stopped going to church after that and started doing my own research and came across Islam. I was instantly triggered back to my earlier years of encountering Muslims and all of things I had been previously told about Islam. The more I read, the more Islam just "fit". It fit who I was at the core. The literature just spoke to me.

So fast forward, I am doing all of this reading and at the time, I was working for an international organization. I am standing in my boss'/ mentor's office (he knew what I was considering at the time) and in walks the most beautiful woman I've ever seen. She was beautiful not because of her physical appearance per se but she was wearing a hijab and the brightest Nur (light) was radiating from her. I had to know who she was! I told my boss I would be right back; turns out she was new to the organization. She must have thought I was crazy running up on her like that. Anyway, I told her that I had been reading about Islam and I was so curious. She was excited to tell me about her way of life. We started meeting daily during lunch and she would answer my questions. Then she invited me to the prayer room to watch her pray and asked if I wanted to pray with her and I did. This went on for about a month and then one day I showed up to work and said to her, "I'm ready". She went to another Muslim brother and the two of them gave me my Shahaadah in the prayer room. Later that week, we went to the mosque and we did it again to make it "official". When I did it in the mosque, there were women in the room that didn't know me from a can of paint, with real tears in their eyes for me. The sisters gathered around me and gave me so many hugs that day, and they were REAL hugs, like you felt the love radiating from them, simply because I was now their sister in Islam. It was in those moments that I realized, I had made an excellent decision for my life. I love Islam- I am not the best Muslim and I struggle on many days but I can tell you that this religion has changed my life, my perspective on life and I would go as far as to say, it saved my life!

All of this happened when I was thirty years old, ten years later, I am still a Muslim (all praises to the Most High) and I still believe that this was THE BEST decision I've ever made in my life.

ZARA

———————x( )x———————

Growing up in Philadelphia, being exposed to Islam wasn't anything foreign. You see Muslims everywhere, in school at work, or walking down the street. Philadelphia has a large Muslim community and the impact of the Muslim culture is very strong in the city. So, for me it wasn't so much that Islam was foreign but more so I didn't know the details; I didn't understand the religion on a deeper level. I became intimately exposed to the religion when I was working on my second novel 'Uptown Princess'. I came across the author by the name of Wasiim. Wasiim was a very talented author and he was also an amazing businessman who really helped me and mentored me through writing. While working with Wasiim, I would just notice how dedicated he was to praying, and the language that he used; not drinking alcohol and not fornicating or engaging in certain behaviors and really trying his absolute best to avoid anything that took him away from his religion. I really admired that discipline and dedication and through Wasiim, I was then introduced to my editor, Muhammed. Muhammed, at the time, was incarcerated and I would send him my manuscript for him to edit because he was absolutely the best editor hands down that I have met so far; an amazingly talented editor. So I would send him my manuscripts and he would always email me back or send me letters, and it was always just in a very pure spirit, very eloquently written, and he too would also include things about the deen. As we continued to work with each other and our relationship grew, I now had two daily influences, Muhammad and Wassim. I just noticed a difference in them versus some other people that were also in my circle of influence. Just by knowing them two, my admiration for Islam began to grow but at the same time, I had a lot of resistance because I didn't want to abandon my Christian faith; I didn't want to abandon my family and my background. And I also didn't want to abandon the truth of what I now knew. But the more I learned about Islam, the more sense it made. It was after that Ramadan, that I was like okay it's time for me to dive into it and learn a little bit more. And even still as I learned, there was a lot of resistance. The more I questioned and learned, the more I rebelled against some of the things I was learning because I didn't want to give up certain aspects of my lifestyle. At the time I hadn't been drinking and I wasn't dating or anything like that, I actually hadn't even gone to church for about eight months just because of where I had moved and it just wasn't convenient to get to my usual church.

So it was kind of just the right timing for me to be taking all this information in, because I was actually open to receive it. One afternoon. I was taking my son to the barber shop he was about, maybe two or three at the time. The barber shop I took him to, his barber was a Muslim; in fact, everyone who worked in the barber shop was Muslim. And if you're from Philadelphia you know that a lot of the barbers in Philadelphia are Muslim. So, at this time, we were sitting in the barber shop, and they were having a discussion about Islam, and I joined in the conversation here there. And the question to me was, "How do you know so much about

the religion, you're not Muslim?" and I said oh because I've studied, I've read about it and I've learned it. So then his barber asked me, "Do you believe that it's the truth?" And I say yes. And then, his barber said well, then why haven't you taken Shahada. And I said, No, I'm not really ready for that right now, but I do plan to do it one day. So, then his barber said, well, it's best for you to go ahead and take it because what happens if you step outside of the barber shop today, you get hit by a car, God forbid, and you die; You'll be responsible for dying without taking your Shahada when you knew the truth. So, wouldn't you rather go ahead and die upon the truth, instead of taking that risk of waiting until another time in the future?

And that really sat with me, I really let that sink in and it kind of touched me in a way that it allowed something within my spirits to click. I still didn't take it right away, but roughly about two weeks later, I fully made the commitment to dive into being Muslim and committing to that decision. So after I had a conversation with my son's barber I called Wasiim and I told him that I was ready to take Shahada. He gave me my Shahaadah over the phone, and that was it. It was almost as if right away I felt like there were some major shifts within me, changing. I went into hijab about two days later, and I didn't even tell my family or my friends or anyone right away. I only told my best friend but I didn't tell any of my family but my sister, at the time we were roommates. So she had witnessed me studying and it wasn't a major surprise to her, but it was definitely a surprise to my parents, and some of my other family members. It was a decision that I had made for myself and that's why I kept it to myself until about three weeks later when I saw them on Thanksgiving, because I knew that if this was something I was going to go all into, I had to keep it close to me and keep it near to me. I didn't want anyone to try to sway me on my decision. And it has been the best decision that I could have made. It has completely changed my life and I'm grateful to have been chosen by Allah to make that choice.

HASAN

———————————————x( )x———————————————

My conversion is like countless other black men's conversion stories. I was introduced to Islam while in prison, like most men who enter prison I was in search of solace. I was 20 years old. Facing a life sentence, so my first choice was Christianity. Being that I grew up in a church, I gravitated towards something that I knew; the bible. During this time, I started studying the bible intensely. While studying, a major question came to mind: Is Ibrahim (Abraham)a Jew or a Christian? No one seemed to be able to answer this question. So, one day, the group of Christians that I studied with got into a debate, with some Muslims. I, being as the bright young man I felt I was, decided to give my opinion and defend my religion. I was giving scripture after scripture to defend my position however, the intellectual part of me was beginning to understand the position that the Muslims were presenting. What they were saying seemed to make sense. They were answering questions that I had but had no answers to. So, I asked them my most burning question, "Who was Abraham?" He in turn asked, "What do you mean by that question?" So I asked, "Was he a Jew or Christian?" And the brother told me he was neither and that he was a Muslim. To be sure that he was correct in his statement, I asked for evidence of that. He then told me it was in his book, the Quran and showed me the following verse, Surat 3 Ayat 67: "...Abraham was neither a Jew or a Christian, but he was a true Muslim (Islamic Monotheism, to worship no but Allah alone) and he was not of the polytheists (worshipping anything other than Allah) and he joined none in worship with Allah. With him producing that evidence to me from a book, made me contemplate very deeply about the direction I needed to go. So I figured, if a book can answer those questions directly, maybe I need to give that book a little more attention. So, the brother and I became friends, we used to talk constantly, about life, religion, manhood and spirituality; and within a week I was taking Shahaadah. This was the summer of 1986, to be exact July 18, 1986.

KAREEM

―――――――――――――――=)( )(=――――――

Kareem's story is presented a lot differently than everyone else's. Below I have included the YouTube link that documents his entire journey to Islam. It's a beautiful and inspiring videography walk through of his story. I pray you enjoy it, just as I did. I pray you enjoyed this entire book and are left feeling full of hope and with a new perspective.

Presenting Kareem Story:

https://youtu.be/AjwkID85FsU

About the Author

Najwa Haamen was born and raised a Muslim in Philadelphia, Pa. Although Najwa has not taken a similar journey as the beautiful people's stories written in this book, the personal journey she has taken to grow into herself as a muslim in America, is one that connets her to so many people, both Muslim and Non- Muslim. She spent over a decade in the healthcare field working as a Surgical Technologist and a Sterile Processing Technician. Najwa is currently the owner of B.E.A.T. Apparel, LLC, an e-commerce retail store. Presenting stylish clothing with a message of affirmation to always be Extraordinary. As well as her niche' based, African inspired boutique on Etsy. As a proud mother of two gorgeous girls, Najwa enjoys spending time with her family and friends when she is not working on her businesses or blossoming into the new realm of Author-hood.

Made in the USA
Coppell, TX
28 November 2020

42343481R00020